BIRD VIEWING AREAS

⑥ Melita/Lyleton Area
⑦ Pelican Lake
⑧ Turtle Mountain Provincial Park
⑨ Spruce Woods Provincial Park
⑩ Pembina River Valley (Windygates)
⑪ LaBarrière Park (Winnipeg)
⑫ Assiniboine Park (Winnipeg)
⑬ Kildonan Park (Winnipeg)
⑭ St. Vital Park (Winnipeg)
⑮ King's Park (Winnipeg)
⑯ Fort Whyte Alive (Winnipeg)
⑰ Oak Hammock Marsh Wildlife Management Area
⑱ Delta Marsh Complex
⑲ St. Ambroise Provincial Park
⑳ Birds Hill Provincial Park
㉑ Winnipeg Beach Provincial Park
㉒ Hecla/Grindstone Provincial Park
㉓ Victoria Beach
㉔ Patricia Beach Provincial Park
㉕ Whiteshell Provincial Park
㉖ Ste. Geneviève Area

① Churchill
② Duck Mountain Provincial Park
③ Riding Mountain National Park
④ Oak Lake/ Plum Marshes
⑤ Whitewater Lake Wildlife Management Area

This guide was produced in collaboration with The Harry J Enns Wetland Discovery Centre at Oak Hammock Marsh and Ducks Unlimited Canada.

A portion of the proceeds from the sale of this guide are returned to The Harry J Enns Wetland Discovery Centre to support their ongoing programs and conservation work. Visit their website at oakhammockmarsh.ca.

Waterford Press produces reference guides that introduce novices to nature, science, survival and outdoor recreation. Product information is featured on the website:
www.waterfordpress.com

Text and illustrations © 2021 by Waterford Press Inc. All rights reserved. Cover images © Shutterstock.
To order, call 800-434-2555.
For permissions, or to share comments, e-mail info@waterfordpress.com.
For information on custom-published products, call 800-434-2555 or e-mail info@waterfordpress.com. 210401

978-1-62005-496-3 $7.95 U.S.

Made in the USA

MANITOBA BIRDS – A Folding Pocket Guide to Familiar Species

A POCKET NATURALIST® GUIDE

MANITOBA BIRDS

A Folding Pocket Guide to Familiar Species

WATERBIRDS & NEARSHORE BIRDS

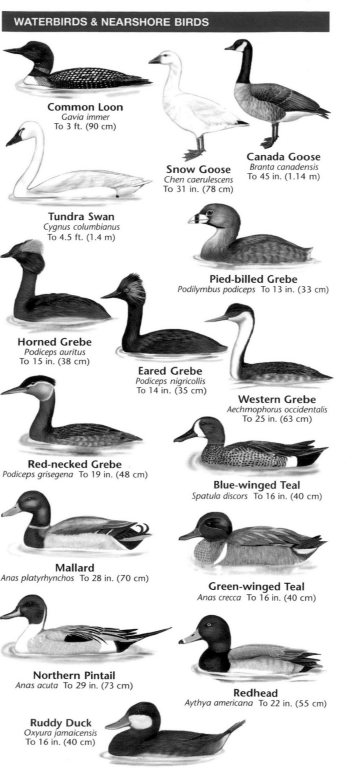

Common Loon
Gavia immer
To 3 ft. (90 cm)

Snow Goose
Chen caerulescens
To 31 in. (78 cm)

Canada Goose
Branta canadensis
To 45 in. (1.14 m)

Tundra Swan
Cygnus columbianus
To 4.5 ft. (1.4 m)

Pied-billed Grebe
Podilymbus podiceps To 13 in. (33 cm)

Horned Grebe
Podiceps auritus
To 15 in. (38 cm)

Eared Grebe
Podiceps nigricollis
To 14 in. (35 cm)

Western Grebe
Aechmophorus occidentalis
To 25 in. (63 cm)

Red-necked Grebe
Podiceps grisegena To 19 in. (48 cm)

Blue-winged Teal
Spatula discors To 16 in. (40 cm)

Mallard
Anas platyrhynchos To 28 in. (70 cm)

Green-winged Teal
Anas crecca To 16 in. (40 cm)

Northern Pintail
Anas acuta To 29 in. (73 cm)

Redhead
Aythya americana To 22 in. (55 cm)

Ruddy Duck
Oxyura jamaicensis
To 16 in. (40 cm)

WATERBIRDS & NEARSHORE BIRDS

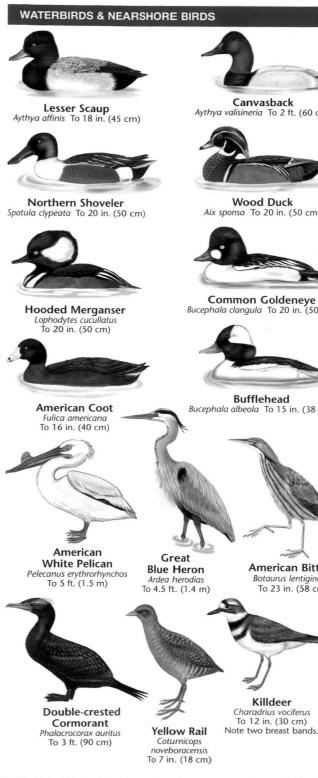

Lesser Scaup
Aythya affinis To 18 in. (45 cm)

Canvasback
Aythya valisineria To 2 ft. (60 cm)

Northern Shoveler
Spatula clypeata To 20 in. (50 cm)

Wood Duck
Aix sponsa To 20 in. (50 cm)

Hooded Merganser
Lophodytes cucullatus
To 20 in. (50 cm)

Common Goldeneye
Bucephala clangula To 20 in. (50 cm)

American Coot
Fulica americana
To 16 in. (40 cm)

Bufflehead
Bucephala albeola To 15 in. (38 cm)

American White Pelican
Pelecanus erythrorhynchos
To 5 ft. (1.5 m)

Great Blue Heron
Ardea herodias
To 4.5 ft. (1.4 m)

American Bittern
Botaurus lentiginosus
To 23 in. (58 cm)

Double-crested Cormorant
Phalacrocorax auritus
To 3 ft. (90 cm)

Yellow Rail
Coturnicops noveboracensis
To 7 in. (18 cm)

Killdeer
Charadrius vociferus
To 12 in. (30 cm)
Note two breast bands.

WATERBIRDS & NEARSHORE BIRDS

Black-crowned Night-Heron
Nycticorax nycticorax
To 28 in. (70 cm)

Sandhill Crane
Antigone canadensis
To 4 ft. (1.2 m)

American Avocet
Recurvirostra americana
To 20 in. (50 cm)

Wilson's Phalarope
Phalaropus tricolor
To 9 in. (23 cm)

Marbled Godwit
Limosa fedoa
To 20 in. (50 cm)

Sora
Porzana carolina
To 10 in. (25 cm)

Willet
Tringa semipalmata
To 17 in. (43 cm)

Wilson's Snipe
Gallinago delicata
To 12 in. (30 cm)

Ring-billed Gull
Larus delawarensis
To 20 in. (50 cm)
Bill has dark ring.

Greater Yellowlegs
Tringa melanoleuca
To 15 in. (38 cm)

Franklin's Gull
Leucophaeus pipixcan
To 14 in. (35 cm)
Bill is reddish.

Herring Gull
Larus argentatus
To 26 in. (65 cm)
Legs are pinkish.

Forster's Tern
Sterna forsteri
To 15 in. (38 cm)

Black Tern
Chlidonias niger
To 10 in. (25 cm)

BIRDS OF PREY

Bald Eagle
Haliaeetus leucocephalus
To 40 in. (1 m)

American Kestrel
Falco sparverius
To 12 in. (30 cm)

Northern Harrier
Circus hudsonius
To 22 in. (55 cm)
Marsh hawk has a white rump.

Red-tailed Hawk
Buteo jamaicensis
To 25 in. (63 cm)

Swainson's Hawk
Buteo swainsoni
To 22 in. (55 cm)
Note dark terminal tail band.

Rough-legged Hawk
Buteo lagopus
To 2 ft. (60 cm)
Note dark banded white tail and dark 'wrists'.

Osprey
Pandion haliaetus
To 2 ft. (60 cm)

Merlin
Falco columbarius
To 14 in. (35 cm)
Tail is heavily banded.

Great Horned Owl
Bubo virginianus
To 25 in. (63 cm)
Call is a resonant –
hoo-oo-oo, hoo-oo.

Northern Hawk Owl
Surnia ulula
To 18 in. (45 cm)

Great Gray Owl
Strix nebulosa
To 33 in. (83 cm)
Large gray owl has a black and white 'bow tie'.

Snowy Owl
Bubo scandiacus
To 27 in. (68 cm)

Short-eared Owl
Asio flammeus
To 17 in. (43 cm)
Call is a high, raspy barking.

Turkey Vulture
Cathartes aura
To 32 in. (80 cm)
Note two-toned underwings.

Ruffed Grouse
Bonasa umbellus
To 19 in. (48 cm)
Note black tail band.

Gray Partridge
Perdix perdix
To 14 in. (35 cm)

Spruce Grouse
Falcipennis canadensis
To 18 in. (45 cm)

Sharp-tailed Grouse
Tympanuchus phasianellus
To 20 in. (50 cm)

Rock Pigeon
Columba livia
To 13 in. (33 cm)

Ruby-throated Hummingbird
Archilochus colubris
To 3.5 in. (9 cm)

Mourning Dove
Zenaida macroura
To 13 in. (33 cm)
Call is a mournful –
ooah-woo-woo-woo.

Belted Kingfisher
Megaceryle alcyon
To 14 in. (35 cm)

Hairy Woodpecker
Dryobates villosus
To 10 in. (25 cm)
The similar hairy woodpecker is larger and has a longer bill.

Downy Woodpecker
Dryobates pubescens
To 6 in. (15 cm)

Yellow-bellied Sapsucker
Sphyrapicus varius
To 9 in. (23 cm)
Drills holes in trees and feeds on the sap and insects that collect there.

Red-headed Woodpecker
Melanerpes erythrocephalus
To 10 in. (25 cm)

Northern Flicker
Colaptes auratus
To 13 in. (33 cm)
Wing and tail linings are yellow.

Least Flycatcher
Empidonax minimus
To 5 in. (13 cm)

Eastern Kingbird
Tyrannus tyrannus
To 8 in. (20 cm)
Note broad white tail band.

Western Kingbird
Tyrannus verticalis
To 8 in. (20 cm)
Note yellowish belly and square-tipped tail.

Yellow-throated Vireo
Vireo flavifrons
To 6 in. (15 cm)

Red-eyed Vireo
Vireo olivaceus
To 6 in. (15 cm)

Canada Jay
Perisoreus canadensis
To 14 in. (35 cm)

Blue Jay
Cyanocitta cristata
To 14 in. (35 cm)

American Crow
Corvus brachyrhynchos
To 22 in. (55 cm)
Call is a distinct – caw.

Common Raven
Corvus corax
To 27 in. (68 cm)
Call is a hoarse croak.

Black-billed Magpie
Pica hudsonia
To 22 in. (55 cm)

Red-breasted Nuthatch
Sitta canadensis
To 4.5 in. (11 cm)

Tree Swallow
Tachycineta bicolor
To 6 in. (15 cm)

White-breasted Nuthatch
Sitta carolinensis
To 6 in. (15 cm)

Black-capped Chickadee
Poecile atricapillus
To 6 in. (15 cm)
Name-saying call is –
chick-a-dee-dee-dee.

Barn Swallow
Hirundo rustica
To 8 in. (20 cm)

House Wren
Troglodytes aedon
To 5 in. (13 cm)

Sedge Wren
Cistothorus platensis
To 4.5 in. (11 cm)
Note white stripes on back and white eyebrow stripe.

Marsh Wren
Cistothorus palustris
To 5 in. (13 cm)
Note white stripes on back and white eyebrow stripe.

Ruby-crowned Kinglet
Regulus calendula
To 4 in. (10 cm)

American Robin
Turdus migratorius
To 11 in. (28 cm)

Swainson's Thrush
Catharus ustulatus
To 7 in. (18 cm)

Hermit Thrush
Catharus guttatus faxoni
To 7 in. (18 cm)
Note rusty tail and spotted breast.

Cedar Waxwing
Bombycilla cedrorum
To 7 in. (18 cm)
Red wing marks look like waxy droplets.

European Starling
Sturnus vulgaris
To 8 in. (20 cm)

Black-and-white Warbler
Mniotilta varia
To 6 in. (15 cm)
Note striped crown.

Gray Catbird
Dumetella carolinensis
To 9 in. (23 cm)
Repetitive call of variable sounds is interspersed with cat-like mew notes.

Mourning Warbler
Geothlypis philadelphia
To 5 in. (13 cm)

Ovenbird
Seiurus aurocapilla
To 6 in. (15 cm)
Distinctive call is –
tea-cher, tea-cher.

Connecticut Warbler
Oporornis agilis
To 6 in. (15 cm)

Common Yellowthroat
Geothlypis trichas
To 5 in. (13 cm)

American Redstart
Setophaga ruticilla
To 5 in. (13 cm)

Magnolia Warbler
Setophaga magnolia
To 5 in. (13 cm)
Note large white wing patch.

Palm Warbler
Setophaga palmarum
To 6 in. (15 cm)

Cape May Warbler
Setophaga tigrina
To 5 in. (13 cm)
Note chestnut cheek.

Northern Parula
Setophaga americana
To 4.5 in. (11 cm)

'Myrtle' Race

'Audubon' Race

Yellow-rumped Warbler
Setophaga coronata
To 6 in. (15 cm)
Note yellow on rump and crown. Throat is yellow or white.

Yellow Warbler
Setophaga petechia
To 5 in. (13 cm)

Rose-breasted Grosbeak
Pheucticus ludovicianus
To 9 in. (23 cm)

American Tree Sparrow
Spizelloides arborea
To 7 in. (18 cm)
Note chestnut cap and small breast spot.

Clay-colored Sparrow
Spizella pallida
To 5 in. (13 cm)

Chipping Sparrow
Spizella passerina
To 5 in. (13 cm)
Note chestnut cap.

Le Conte's Sparrow
Ammodramus leconteii
To 5 in. (13 cm)

Savannah Sparrow
Passerculus sandwichensis
To 6 in. (15 cm)
Note yellowish eyebrow.

Nelson's Sparrow
Ammodramus nelsoni
To 5 in. (13 cm)

Song Sparrow
Melospiza melodia
To 7 in. (18 cm)
Note central breast spot.

Swamp Sparrow
Melospiza georgiana
To 6 in. (15 cm)
Note red cap and white throat.

White-throated Sparrow
Zonotrichia albicollis
To 7 in. (18 cm)
Note white throat and yellow spot in front of eye.

Harris's Sparrow
Zonotrichia querula
To 8 in. (20 cm)

White-crowned Sparrow
Zonotrichia leucophrys
To 8 in. (20 cm)
White crown is bordered by black stripes.

Grasshopper Sparrow
Ammodramus savannarum
To 5 in. (13 cm)
Chunky, buff-colored sparrow has a short tail.

Baird's Sparrow
Ammodramus bairdii
To 5 in. (13 cm)

Snow Bunting
Plectrophenax nivalis
To 8 in. (20 cm)

Indigo Bunting
Passerina cyanea
To 6 in. (15 cm)

Dark-eyed Junco
Junco hyemalis
To 7 in. (18 cm)

Common Grackle
Quiscalus quiscula
To 14 in. (35 cm)

Red-winged Blackbird
Agelaius phoeniceus
To 9 in. (23 cm)

Western Meadowlark
Sturnella neglecta
To 9 in. (23 cm)

Bobolink
Dolichonyx oryzivorus
To 8 in. (20 cm)

Yellow-headed Blackbird
Xanthocephalus xanthocephalus
To 11 in. (28 cm)

Brown-headed Cowbird
Molothrus ater
To 7 in. (18 cm)

Baltimore Oriole
Icterus galbula
To 8 in. (20 cm)

House Sparrow
Passer domesticus
To 6 in. (15 cm)

Pine Siskin
Spinus pinus
To 5 in. (13 cm)

American Goldfinch
Spinus tristis
To 5 in. (13 cm)

Common Redpoll
Acanthis flammea
To 5 in. (13 cm)

House Finch
Haemorhous mexicanus
To 6 in. (15 cm)

Evening Grosbeak
Coccothraustes vespertinus
To 8 in. (20 cm)